FORCED SWIMMING TEST
ESSAYS ON FAMILY, MENTAL HEALTH, NEURODIVERGENCE AND MEDICATION

CW01508340

Eva Aldea is a writer and artist, lecturer and editor. Her first novel *Singapore* (Holland House Books, 2023), and her book in progress, *Stockholm*, explore migration and belonging. She has written about the experience of taking nude selfies as a way of exploring body image and the gaze in the pamphlet *Possible Selves* (Intergraphia Books, 2024). Eva is interested in the relationship between diagnoses, physical and psychological, and writing, and edits writers' reflections on how these affect their craft on the website *Dx: Diagnosis and Writing*. Eva teaches literature, critical theory and creative writing. She is also freelance Editor in Chief at W.R.K.S Games.

Also by Eva Aldea

CONTENTS

ISBN: 978-1-917617-15-4

Cover designed by Aaron Kent

Edited and Typeset by Aaron Kent

Broken Sleep Books Ltd
PO BOX 102
Llandysul
SA44 9BG

Forced Swimming Test

Eva Aldea

Broken Sleep Books

Foreword

The four essays in *Forced Swimming Test* were written over the span of several years, two essays before and two after my neurodivergence assessment and diagnosis. Like a ruminating mind they loop around, returning to the same topics over and over. But by way of this repetition, they also progress towards an acceptance of being someone that "definitely approaches the world differently than others," as my diagnosing psychiatrist put it. Perhaps I am, but there are enough people that, like me, think and feel differently about the world to make me wonder at the usefulness of calling us divergent.

Those people who approach the world differently have always been around me and finding a new language to explain and to share our experiences has been a revelation and a relief. Sometimes it has been a way to articulate our profound differences and coming to terms with the misunderstandings and hurt these have caused.

I am immensely grateful to those of you who have been there, even when I have not, and that have always stayed ready to listen to me, to comfort me, to discuss and disagree, and to cry and to laugh with me. This is for you.

I hope that both those with a mind like mine and "others" find a point of connection in these essays, whether that is a recognition of having struggled through some of the same things, a better understanding of those who have, or an insight into the philosophical and political implications of how we approach mental health in our society.

TL;DR:

You will never be happy.

But you will feel happiness again.

— London, 2025

Numbness, Anxiety, Anger, Grief

IN the hospital, I am not yet angry. I haven't realised that anger is available to me. And the grief that will eventually hit me is far off still—when someone has survived it is not the time to grieve. In fact, I don't feel as much as you'd think, apart from a sinking sense in my stomach of "this isn't happening again," immediately replaced by a cold brick of, "what do I do now?" I go into problem-solving mode, in which I am not angry at anyone, neither the doctors, nor my mother, nor myself. I am not even anxious, that comes later. Now I am just trying to figure out how to fix my mum.

My mother is in a room in the medical intensive care unit in *Södersjukhuset* in Stockholm. There are four beds in the room, two on each side of a central nurses' station that looks like a space-ship command console with waist-high desks. As I walk in, a nurse in blue scrubs and white clogs is sitting just outside the station, with crossed legs and a kind smile. The room is cosy compared to the general ward I found my mother in last week. My mother, in one of the beds, looks tiny. She is trembling. The smiling nurse gets up and passes me the stool she's been sitting on, while she goes to tend to another patient. I sit next to my mother, and I don't know what to say or how to feel. I do know she was brought here by ambulance in the night after having taken an overdose of antidepressants, because she told me so herself when she called earlier that morning.

I am not yet angry that nobody from the psychiatric ward contacted me when she did this to herself. I am not yet angry that my mother's first suicide attempt was not taken seriously, or that they gave her enough free rein on the ward to allow her to try again. I am not yet angry at the system for not assessing or treating her in any meaningful way after her first attempt, except medically, or at the psychiatric services for merely providing a warehouse for those who harm themselves or others until they are sufficiently pacified by meds or time or boredom to be let out again.

I am not yet angry with my mother. I am not yet angry that she stowed away a hundred tablets of a common antidepressant while she was out on permission with me for the weekend. I am not yet angry that when I then talked to her about the previous suicide attempt a few days before, what she said me made me think that she was persuaded that she could be helped, that we could sort her life out somehow, together. I am not yet angry that she deliberately misled me on the way back to the psychiatric hospital, when she said she was just going to pop into the little corner shop across the road, which was when she hid the meds in some bushes to evade the bag search on admission.

I am not yet angry with myself for being so gullible. I am not yet angry with myself for not realising how bad things had got with my mother. I am not yet angry that there is nothing I can do to help her.

There is a plastic bag on the floor by the bed, with a pair of institutional joggers that I recognise as the ones my mother was wearing the day before. They are stamped with the local psychiatry provider's logo. The trousers are wet, but clean, as if someone has rinsed and wrung them. A wave of sadness and shame washes over me. My mother denies that the joggers are hers. An overdose of SSRIs makes you go into convulsions and fits, so she may not remember. Or she may choose not to remember. It is not the first time I am not sure whether my mother is lying or mistaken. I have often wondered if she changes facts because she needs to, if they then become her truth, or whether she cannot tell the difference, whether her reality is simply not the same as mine.

In a voice still shaking from all the serotonin in her system she tells me that it is her turn to die of depression. That her mother, who lived through the war and brought up two children in post-war communist Poland, died of depression. My grandmother was seventy-nine when she died and now, having turned seventy-four, my mother says it is her turn. That I need to put her in a psychiatric institution or a care home, because that is the way things are going to go.

At least this time around, she recognises me. When I flew in from London a week ago, after her first suicide attempt, she looked at me with confusion and said in a thin, childlike voice, "I promise I will try my best to get better, doctor." I was stunned, it was so not like her, the *her* she was to me: determined and straight-talking. "It's me, mum, your daughter." I vividly remember the red wool jumper I was wearing; I can't put it on without thinking of this moment. It took her a beat, but then I saw realisation in her eyes. I don't recall what we said to each other, but her voice was her own again. The same voice my mother uses now, the second time around in hospital, when she tells me about my grandmother and depression and death.

Before she is discharged back to the psychiatric ward, she is seen by the hospital's on-call psychiatrist. I am asked to attend with her permission. We are in a small room: muted grey walls and muted green upholstery. My mother is in a wheelchair wrapped in a pale-yellow hospital blanket. She repeats what she has told me. What my mother leaves out of the story is that she left her native Poland with her husband and infant at a time when her father was dying of cancer and that she never saw him again, that her mother suffered from dementia for years and lived with my mother's sister and her family in a small flat for many of those years. There are layers of trauma and guilt behind my mother's words, but nobody asks any further questions.

The best the on-call psychiatrist can do is to berate my mother for what she has done to me. "Look how upset your daughter is, you need to be strong so that you don't cause her anymore pain." Even though I don't know then what I have since come to know, this strikes me as the most preposterous thing to say to someone who has just tried to take their own life. You can't guilt someone out of suffering. Even when anger floods me later, wave after wave, I know that my anger is not going to heal my mother. Why isn't anybody asking what brought her here? Why isn't anybody asking why she wants to kill herself? Even now that my anger has turned to profound sadness, I know my grief isn't going to heal her either.

The anxiety comes after the numbness, but before the anger and the grief. An all-consuming worry that hits me as soon as I wake up. My heart starts racing and I feel short of breath. I can't sit still. I can't eat. I can't think of anything else but what I need to do to fix my mother. My mother who is suffering the same overwhelming anxiety. It is as if over the last two months, by some kind of process of osmosis, my mother's mental illness has been transferred to me. It is this debilitating anxiety she feels every morning that has made her want to die. She'd told me of the anxiety about a year before her suicide attempts, and I encouraged her to seek help from a doctor, maybe a therapist. My father had died a couple of years prior, and she'd finally stopped working as a consultant paediatrician after a time of semi-retirement. Her life had changed dramatically, and she was getting noticeably physically older, too. It would have been a lot to deal with. But she claimed she didn't need a therapist: "I already know what they're going to say."

Neither antidepressants in increased doses, nor benzodiaze-pines helped. About six months before she tried to take her own life, she told me she wanted to die. That her anxiety was so intense she could not stand it anymore. How does one reply to one's moth-er saying that she wants to die? "I don't want you to die," I said, but I also told her I was unsure of how to deal with what she had just given voice to. Again, I tried to persuade her to see someone professional. "I am your daughter, I don't know how to help you. Please find someone who can." She still didn't get a therapist, and any further changes in medication made no difference. I told my husband I needed to go and see my mother and figure out what I could do to help her, the day before she stopped responding to me. I called a neighbour who found her in the conservatory, very sedated but vaguely responsive. Paramedics discovered empty blister packs of ninety oxazepam in her bin. Turns out benzos are a lot less toxic than you think. She just had to sleep it off in hospital. That's when my mother put on the mask meant for her doctor for me by mistake. I should have realised then how I had watched her perform these roles before, felt embarrassment at her always having to pretend, but I just thought everyone's parents make them cringe.

It is a rude awakening, after my mother's suicide attempts, that the wheels of mental and social care grind slowly even in Scandinavia. My mother is held in a psychiatric ward, more securely this time, only for as long as it is clear she can't function on her own. Then she is encouraged to get back to her life, just as it is. Getting care and a crisis plan takes months. She has more weekends at home, with me or without, when I can do nothing but hope she'll be fine. There are emergency return trips to the ward for days and weeks. Then there is a handover to an outpatient psychiatrist she sees occasionally, together with more frequent contact with a mental health nurse. Initially, on the ward, she has no talking therapy. I am informed that suicidal patients have to be medicated before they are ready for that. Later, as an outpatient, she receives three weeks of cognitive behavioural therapy.

All this time my mother is adamant that she does not need therapy, that if the meds don't work it is because she is incurably mentally ill, and that she needs to live in an institution. Her idea of what this would be like is vague: somewhere where she doesn't need to be anxious anymore because there are people to take care of her. Where her meals and her meds are served on schedule. Where she can sit in a room with others, but she has her own space. Where there is a panic button in her room.

The happiest I see her during this time is in the psychiatric ward, which ticks all of these boxes. She talks and jokes with the other patients. Perhaps I can't blame the staff for thinking she wasn't really suicidal. But in her room, when I try to talk to her alone, she is often agitated and grows more so as I suggest ways to get her well and out of the ward. "I can't. I'm so lonely. I am so anxious." In my view, she doesn't have to be. I can't understand why since my father's death she's increasingly isolated herself whilst complaining of solitude. She's never been particularly social, but I'd always assumed my father was the driving force behind their introverted lives. Why does she not engage in her interests, see the neighbours that invite her, spend time with old friends? "Because I am too anxious." It becomes increasingly clear that she is suffering social anxiety in some form. I have never seen my mother as a shy or fearful person. Most of her life, as far as I knew, she didn't care what people thought about her. She went ahead and did what she wanted: worked, gardened, travelled the world. And in the common room of the psychiatric ward, I see glimpses of that old self of hers. "That's because in here I don't have to worry that I am weird, everyone is," she tells me.

After my anxiety has abated, the anger comes. It creeps in during the years that I spend trying to find a solution for my mother, trying to make her happy again. Anger at the lack of professional and institutional support and at my own continual failure. But mostly, anger at my mother. It blossoms like a toxic cloud. It has always been there, unrecognised, not yet distilled into resentment. It existed as hurt in childhood, it floated around as irritation in adolescence, and came to fruition as frustration in adulthood. Finally, it became raw anger: at her trying to kill herself, at her betrayal with the meds that weekend, at her telling me she'd worried more about the dog than me when she tried to die, at her inability to accept the facts of her life, and her stubborn refusal to do what everyone tells her would make her better.

Everyone—which is mostly me because she doesn't see many other people, sometimes her mental health nurse, and for a time the private psychotherapist I nag her into seeing—tells her to get out more, be active, see people, do things, take an interest. She makes small attempts but then says she can't. People annoy her. She takes no pleasure in anything. "It's the depression," she says, "it's incurable." She keeps insisting she should live in an old people's home, but she is not ill enough to qualify for a place in Sweden, where there are no private ones. For a few months she moves to a nursing home in Poland, but there she gets bored. "It is stupefying sitting in a home," she says. Of course it is, she's an intelligent woman, who needs intelligent human interaction.

She returns to her house in Sweden. This time, over a year after her suicide attempts and after another stay in the psychiatric ward, she is given carers who look in on her twice a day, a cooked meal delivered once a day, and a shopping service and company on a walk once or twice a week. But the carers are no substitute for friends or activities. "I'm so lonely," she keeps on telling me, but when she sees people, she is sullen and uncommunicative. She declines the walks and dismisses the shoppers: "They bought unsalted butter!" She doesn't want to go out, she doesn't want to meet new people, she doesn't want to socialise with people she knows. She appears to barely tolerate a neighbour that comes around for ten minutes every evening. When the neighbour goes away on holiday, my mother says she misses her. My anger blooms.

As my mother's depression is seen to be drug resistant, she is offered alternative treatments. She refuses trans-cranial magnetic stimulation, saying she has read it can make depression worse. I look into TMS and find no evidence for this. My anger balloons. Sometimes I get so angry with her I shout at her, tell her she doesn't want to get better, that she has decided she is depressed and that she's always been stubborn, and it is her own fault. She gets tearful and withdrawn, she ends up sitting mute and staring, her mouth half open in an attitude of catatonia. I don't know if I'm more angry at her or myself or the *they* that aren't there to help either of us.

My mother does not comprehend why I am angry at her. A few months after her suicide attempts, she asked me about those days, because she couldn't quite remember things. When she saw that I was upset talking about it, she said, "why are you still angry at me when I have apologised?" And I realised she did not understand. To my mother, saying sorry—and she did say sorry sincerely— cancelled my need for anger. This is her logic.

The anger I feel with her for trying to kill herself is eclipsed by the anger at her inability to understand my emotions, then and now: what appears to me as her life-long—my whole life—incapacity for empathy. This is something I have never been able to square with her profession. She used to work with the most underprivileged in her youth, the Roma population in Romania. If she could listen to the ailments of poor kids, why did she never listen to me?

One of my abiding memories of my mother is of her back walking away from me as I am begging her to wait. I am small, and I've had to stop, I don't remember why. My mother doesn't slow down and doesn't turn around. I expect this isn't a real memory, but one that has been amalgamated and sharpened with time. Since moving away from home, I went travelling with my mother almost every year in an attempt to make things work between us. We visited some beautiful, faraway places together. She used to drive me mad taking photos or smoking or walking where it was prohibited. In Bhutan, where smoking is forbidden nationwide, she sneaked off to have fags like a teenager on a school-trip. When I asked her not to, she first refused, then hid from me.

I still don't understand her compulsion to break rules like that, but I think it has to do with the lack of a logical reason. She never deliberately hurt anyone, and it is true that in a corner of the Himalayas, who cares if an old woman has a smoke behind the hotel kitchens. I cared, illogically, for nobody saw. I felt mortified at the thought that somebody that she photographed without asking permission may feel offended, that those whose carefully manicured lawn she trod on may be slighted. But my hurt did not come from social embarrassment, but rather from the fact that even though I explained to her that it made *me* uncomfortable, she did not care. My upset was not reason enough for her. I don't think she ever realised how much she hurt me over such trivial things. I think if she had realised, she would have apologised. Instead, she would often later take offence over something *I* didn't fully understand, and I would think she was getting even. In Bhutan she said loudly to someone else in our tour group, "this was my dream trip, and my daughter has ruined it."

One night I dream that my mother is cutting off my hand to give to someone else. I am in hospital, due to have an operation on my foot. She is my doctor and brusquely jabs my vein to draw blood. When I look down my arm is in two pieces. I scream, but she calmly explains that since I am getting a new foot it is only fair that I give a hand. "How can you take my right hand?" I shout at her, already wondering if I can learn to write with my left. It matters little that severing someone's hand is monstrous, this is her logic: there will be no discussion.

"Keep up!" The memory of my mother walking away is there somewhere, but now she is walking to work, and I don't want her to go, I want her to stay at home with me, but of course she can't. She has to work. She has to work a lot, day and night, to qualify as a consultant.

In the logic of the dream, I am transported in the back of a large black car, someone who is my father driving, mother and I in the back. Playing the role of the child, I cry and pout. My hand is missing. As I arrive in the hospital where the operation on my foot is to take place I am strapped down on a gurney. I am a man, a man who is being dismissed as quarrelsome and mad. I suffer small interventions and indignities while being wheeled through the corridors: labels and sensors are applied to my body. I try to explain that there had been no reason to take my right arm, but I am gagged. They look at me and say I will need sedation if I carry on. I wake up, full of fear and anger and helplessness.

In this dream, I am both recreating my own deep frustration

in the face of my mother's logical lack of empathy for my emotions, and somehow inhabiting what I imagine is her own sense of impotence against the mental anguish that is now gripping her, leaving her the powerless patient of therapies she is convinced won't work.

I guess as a medical doctor one sometimes has to make monstrous decisions. What heals often also hurts. I used to wonder if my mother was a good doctor because she had this ability, or if she became so inured to suffering at work that she could no longer extend her empathy beyond her logic. As a child I relished being ill because that was when she gave me her attention. I still love going to the doctor. It's not that my mother never understood my pain. She often told me a story of how I wouldn't stop crying after pinching my toe in a door when I was a toddler. She had been distraught and biked about with me in the child seat for hours to calm me down. It's just that when she couldn't understand my feelings, she seemed unable to acknowledge them.

In her world, my mother once said, she had to be hard to get ahead. It made sense, as a woman, of her age, in her profession. My father was an emotional man, and quite volatile when he was younger. When I found her smoking in Bhutan when she'd said she wouldn't and I called her a liar, she told me she'd got used to lying to get around my father's anger. It was such a strange response to me, then. In his later years my father let her do whatever she wanted. "There is no point in making her upset," he said.

My mother sometimes expressed the opinion that you have to manipulate people, that you need to calculate what to give to people "to keep them interested, to make them stick around." This struck me as untrue when I finally developed my own friendships and relationships. My best friends don't expect anything, remain even when I myself am absent. But I am aware of my own bias for honesty: I hate hiding my emotions, and I often feel like I say too much. I have perhaps found friends in those that allow me to do so.

So many times, I have wondered why my mother feels the need to lie, to perform and to manipulate. I overhear her speaking to one of the visiting carers in the shaky voice of a much older woman, and when I ask her why, she says she is afraid the care will be withdrawn if she seems "too well." In different ways both my mother and I are afraid of being abandoned.

I finally persuade my mother to go and talk to someone, on the condition that we initially see the therapist together. In one of these common sessions my mental health in childhood is raised. I feel both remorse and relief saying that I don't think my parents were able to deal with my sensitivity and anxiety. My mother balks at this. "You were a school refuser," she says, using a Swedish term that she must have got from the family counselling service we had gone to at the time, a term that indicates an emotional refusal rather than truancy. "I let you stay home one day every term," she continues with exasperation. She had found a solution. I see my mother's confusion in that therapy session. I feel her pain when she hears that I believe she had failed. She phones me up afterwards and asks if I think our mother-daughter relationship is bad, because she doesn't. I don't know what to say, I never imagined anyone could see our relationship as good. All those times I have tried to explain why I was so upset to her; she didn't even register it.

So, with time my anger towards my mother becomes tinged by sadness and the realisation of loss. Six months after the common session, I see the therapist on my own with my mother's consent. The therapist tells me she thinks my mother will never be able to understand my emotions. "Is there perhaps another diagnosis?" the therapist asks, meaning aside from anxiety and depression. In this moment I feel like things start falling into place, and a great big wave of grief washes over me. Grief for having been so hurt and so angry, and grief for my mother: for the life that has led her here, and the life she has been left with.

Almost three years after her suicide attempts my mother is diagnosed with high functioning autism at the age of seventy-seven. The investigation is prompted by me. Initially I am surprised that my mother agrees, and I don't know if it is better care or a confirmation of her incurability that she is after. For her, the diagnosis hasn't made any difference: not to the state of her mental health, nor the help she receives. It has come too late.

To me, her autism explains so many things. It is a relief to know that my mother didn't hurt me on purpose. I used to wonder why she refused to see my side; I'd spend days thinking about how I could explain my point of view to her and worrying that I would make her upset in some way I didn't understand. Could things have been different between us?

It's not just the stubbornness and the rigidity and the social awkwardness and the inability to understand the emotions of others unless they were contextually clear to her, and all the other stereotypically "autistic" traits that I understand now. I also see how much she suffered, and how much she hid, constantly. The time when she stopped speaking for a few days when I was about eleven must have been due to autistic burnout. I cannot help but think that what she is experiencing today is not surprising, considering the amount of effort it took her to exist in the world. It is like she has finally run out of energy to try to fit in with neurotypical life. The determination I knew in her was a survival strategy, her apparent lack of interest in others' view of her, a mask. She performed a persona, confident and strong, for so many years, just to be able to take part in society.

I'd like to imagine that if she had been aware, if there had been a space for neurodivergence in the world seventy-odd years ago, it would have made life less hard for her. Maybe it would have made parenting easier for her, too, and being her child easier for me. It's difficult to admit to, but I used to think—still do—that my mother should never have had kids. She once said to me, "I could have been a professor if it wasn't for you." Is there a world in which she could have been the mother I needed and still have been herself?

I have not yet reached a resolution between my anger and grief. I visit my mother regularly—it is the only thing I can do—and the anger wells up again, instantaneously, when I arrive at her house. She greets me, briefly hugs me, then goes on with her business as if I was not even there. She lives according to a schedule she no longer has any interest in deviating from. She has withdrawn from the world, from life, making her space smaller and smaller, discarding anything that needs her attention and triggering her anxiety. She has emptied out my childhood home, retaining only the bare necessities, only things that serve a purpose.

I was distressed when my father was dying, and she got rid of his clothes as soon as he was taken to hospice. To me, to do this before he was even dead was inconceivable, but I guess it was her way of dealing with a grief she did not know how to handle. "I lost him a long time ago," she said, and she was right, he stopped being who he was months before he died. I lost her a long time ago, too. But I have not been able to stop hoping she would somehow become the mother I always needed.

I am sitting on my mother's settee, and she is lying next to me, her eyes closed. I am reading Fernando Pessoa's *Book of Disquiet*: "To fall asleep! To have peace! To be an abstract consciousness that's conscious only of breathing peacefully, without a world..." Like Pessoa, I know that relief, and I understand why my mother spends a lot of her time in this kind of half-sleep. As I look at her my anger reveals itself as grief.

To me, hers is a bare life, but I could accept it if she wasn't in so much pain. She still tells me how anxious she is, how depressed she feels, and I can't even tell her that there is help to be had. Help to understand herself enough to be able to find a way not to suffer, and live. What grieves me the most is that she may not have been where she is now, had she received better, more appropriate mental health care, in the past and recently.

Her anxiety and depression in response to the loss of the two great certainties in her life, her work and her husband, are understandable for any human being and almost inevitable in the context of her autism. The routine of work, and the social interaction guided by predictable codes that it provided, must have been invaluable to her. She is not a woman without empathy. As a doctor, a very good one, she is full of compassion for others, but I think she needs a theoretical and practical scaffold to hang it on, and medicine provided such a structure. I also wonder if her so called "lack of empathy" or "inability to understand emotions" was not something she had to develop to protect herself—that hardness she spoke about. She always said she'd been a shy, anxious and sensitive child. So, who she was as a child is as different to who she was as an adult, as the shut-down woman she has become. And yet, she is not without the same need for human connection as all of us. The loss of a life-partner is devastating for anyone. My father had his own troubles, and I don't know what brought and kept my parents together, but they clearly worked out a mode of existing as a couple. Towards the end of his life, my father provided my mother with that which she is sorely missing now. A gentle companionship, with no demand on the kind of interaction she finds difficult: social and emotionally unpredictable.

My anger lingers, but it is mostly anger on behalf of my

mother. Anger that neurodivergence was never even considered in her mental health assessment, and that the treatment options she was offered were at best ineffective, and at worst damaging. I am no expert, I am simply listening to neurodivergent voices out there, but mental health care tailored to neurodivergent people seems woefully inadequate. The cognitive therapy that is these days reflexively doled out to those who present with anxiety and depression, is often not applicable to autistic people, for whom the imperative to just get out there and try new things, socialise in groups and meet new people comes with challenges that cannot be easily overcome. If you have sensory processing issues—my mother often complains of smells and of how things "look ugly"— or if reading body language and other social cues is exhausting—my mother often zones out mid-conversation—or if you're constantly told off for doing things you shouldn't—like my mother was by me—then trying this interaction that you fear, which in most non-neurodivergent people would be revealed as "not so bad after all," does nothing but confirm and increase your anxiety.

If you are lucky enough to be offered or able to afford other talking therapies, much depends on the awareness of the therapist. I recently saw a diagram showing the overlap between autism and alexithymia—the inability to identify and express emotions— and I was struck by the complexity of what a diagnosis of neurodivergence means. Not all autistic persons have alexithymia. My mother does. Psychotherapy with alexithymia is challenging. At least my mother's therapist had the skill to understand that, even if she didn't know how to adjust her methods to the needs of an autistic person.

What remains readily on offer is psychiatric medication. Many autistic people with "uncontrollable" anxiety, including my mother, are treated with anti-psychotics, because these reduce "anti-social" behaviours. That is, in my mother's case, behaviour that sees her in psychiatric care, where all efforts are made to make her "independent" again. Solutions between the ward and the home are few and far between, because they are costly to run well. So, my mother is at home, she is alone, and she is medicated. I believe psychiatric medication is lifesaving, but I cannot but wonder if her life is so limited partly because she is sedated. No other solutions are available.

The grief that overtakes me then, after the numbness and anxiety and anger, is that I can't help my mother. As I watch her doze on the settee next to me, I am sorry that I pushed on her so many solutions that were inappropriate. I am sorry that I am even trying to "solve" her, when her problem is that she has lived her whole life in a society that does not understand or acknowledge her needs. I am so very sorry that because she has lived in this society, she cannot even understand herself. The safe space she made at great cost in this world and held on to with such strength has disappeared. I am not sure she has the energy left to create a new space, or, that she, after a lifetime of masking to herself and the world, can accept the space she needs.

Forced Swimming Test

TWO *adjacent rooms are used in the forced swimming test: the waiting room and the procedure room. There are two sessions, twenty-four hours apart: the pre-test, lasting fifteen minutes, and the test, lasting five. The subjects are taken to the waiting room half an hour prior to the sessions and allowed to eat and drink. There is no food in the procedure room.*

Clear cylinders are filled with water at a temperature of 23 degrees Celsius, one for each subject, and the depth is adjusted so the subjects cannot reach the bottom. The cylinders are separated with dark screens.

At the start of the procedure the subjects are placed in the cylinders. When the time for the pre-test or test has elapsed, the subjects are taken out of the cylinders, returned to the waiting room and monitored during recovery.

I sat down on the curb and cried. Silently at first, then with increasing intensity, until I couldn't breathe. I was sixteen and the feeling that I couldn't go to school, couldn't take another step, and couldn't exist through another day was too strong. All I wanted, as I sat on the side of the pavement in the spring sunshine with my knees pulled up to my face, was to be a blade of grass. One of the many identical thin green leaves growing out of the ground, thinking nothing.

I had got into the international high school I wanted, I had met my first boyfriend, I lived in a green suburb of Stockholm. There was nothing wrong. Maybe that's why it was so frightening, because there was no reason why I should feel this way: like the sheer act of existing was more than I could bear. Pain and exhaustion extended through every bit of me, neither all in my head nor just in my body. Somehow, I made my way back to my house and called my mother. She told me to stay at home and go to bed. It was just what I needed to be told. I hid under the covers and fell asleep to escape it all.

Behaviour in the pre-test is not coded. Behaviour in the test is coded as follows:

- *"Swimming" for movement allowing consistent buoyancy in water.*
- *"Struggling/Climbing" [a.k.a. "Thrashing"] for movements breaking the surface of the water, attempts to escape the cylinder.*
- *"Immobile" for floating without movements except those necessary to keep head above water.*

I sit down at my desk and write. My thoughts are racing, but I can harness that speed. I write. Chaos becomes connections. I write. I am anxious, but I feel alive. I become exhausted. I rest. Then, I write again. I write more and more easily and more furiously than I have done before. Furiously. Like I am making up for lost time. I am forty-six, and thirty years after I fell asleep in my teenage room wishing to be a single blade of grass, three things have happened over the course of twelve months:

○ I have found a literary agent and a publisher for my first novel.

○ I have been diagnosed with chronic fatigue syndrome/myalgic encephalomyelitis.

○ I have got a new psychiatrist and changed my antidepressant medication.

It was the first time, that time when I was sixteen, that I took psychiatric medication, although it is possible that I had been given something to calm me down in the worst moments of my childhood anxiety. I had never been a happy child, beset by fear and sadness for as long as I can remember. That time when I was sixteen, my mother—a paediatrician—prescribed alprazolam, a common benzodiazepine tranquilliser, for two weeks. I spent those weeks in bed, drifting in and out of a dreamy state. I spoke to my boyfriend on the phone, the handset with that electrics-in-plastic smell nestled in my pillow. The curly phone cord pulling itself straight as it reached across the room was the only thing mooring me as I floated beyond the reach of existential pain.

A few years later when I started university in the United Kingdom, I was overcome by the pain of becoming an adult, of living away from home in a different country, of falling in and out of love. I was sitting against the cold walls of the small telephone room in the basement of my halls, crying. My head against my knees again. That smell of old telephone again. This time my mother prescribed the most common type of antidepressants, selective serotonin reuptake inhibitors or SSRIs, which was also what she was taking for her depression.

You may wonder why my mother was the giver of psychiatric care, but at that time I did not. A certain sensitivity to the condition called life ran in our family. For a long time, I felt grateful that what we called depression was openly talked about in our family. Highly educated Eastern European migrants to Sweden in the late 1970s, my mother and father had done well. They spoke the language, held good jobs, owned a house in a middle-class suburb. But they never belonged, and neither did I. For many years I thought it was because we were foreign, but now I'm not so sure.

My parents wore their functional mental illness as a secret badge, a sign of what they had overcome to get this far. Or perhaps it was a talisman to protect against the sense of failure of having got no further. It was something that set us apart, suffering and superior. It was easier for my parents to blame heredity and a cruel world, than to face the past traumas that I later saw stretching like mirrors within mirrors through the generations. Both my parents were on antidepressants. I know they had attended private therapy and family counselling, singly, together, and with me, because I remember my sense of resentment towards the strangers in the bare rooms who talked to my parents about their daughter. I do not remember what they said. So, when the world proved too much to bear, my mother diagnosed and treated me. It was her way of protecting me.

Based on the learned helplessness theory of depression, as postulated by Seligman in the sixties following experiments electroshocking dogs, Porsolt et al. hypothesised that increasing periods of immobility induced by prolonged exposure to an aversive situation from which there is no escape reflected a state of lowered mood or behavioural despair. Porsolt et al. predicted that immobility would be reduced by antidepressants as well as other treatments generally effective in alleviating depression.

The meds weren't a cure. Every year I'd have a number of episodes of what I would name depression—sometimes triggered by events, sometimes without explanation.

To this day, it always begins in the same way, with anxiety: my thoughts speed up, relentlessly going round the same tracks, winding my chest up tighter and tighter, dropping a stone in my stomach, making my heart beat so fast I can feel it inside of me pushing against my ribs. In this state I am convinced that my life depends on resolving the knots in my brain, or else this mental pain that is so physical, like a knife turning in my chest, will go on forever and ever and ever. The worst thing about that level of anxiety is not that you think you'll die, but that you believe that you will continue dying without end.

The anxiety leads to a state of depression, an exhaustion so profound that I can only lie in bed and stare at the wall. The pain of depression is duller, heavier and more physically debilitating than that of anxiety. When in the grip of the worst anxiety I cannot sit still, in the grip of depression I cannot move. It seems impossible that any task, however small, will be achievable again. Perhaps it is a coping mechanism, a biological process ensuring survival in the face of the unsustainable energy expenditure of anxiety. My body and mind rest in the cocoon that a depressive state enforces, one of minimal interaction or stimulation. The whiter the wall I am staring at, the better. Eventually, I find the will to get out of bed, to start doing all those things they call self-care. And I am fine—until next time.

I wish I could say that this became a natural cycle, something I learned to accept and live through without antidepressants. But the truth is that this is a cycle that repeats itself with a tolerable interval and resolves itself in a time frame that I can live with, only when I am on medication. I am not sure what would happen without it: I have never been able to stand the pain long enough to find out.

Further experiments undertaken by Porsolt et al. showed that the duration of immobility in subjects was reduced by various kinds of antidepressant medication, and also by electroconvulsive shock, REM sleep deprivation, and enrichment of the environment. In addition, most treatments that reduced immobility in the forced swimming test left activity in an open field reduced or unaffected. It was concluded that antidepressant effects could be distinguished from the effects of other non-antidepressant treatments such as psychostimulants or tranquillisers, which either increased or decreased open field activity.

My need for sleep has been greater than most people's all my adult life. Almost every day I need a nap, a full night's sleep isn't enough. Half a day of life makes me exhausted, I need to lie down to rest, I need to switch my mind off, to not be—just for a little while. Some days I need to never wake up.

Initially, I treated SSRIs like headache pills, a symptomatic treatment that could be increased and decreased with need. A treatment I could stop. But whenever I stopped the antidepressants, after some time I'd need them again. A few years after university I had a formal psychiatric assessment. I recall several people in a bare room, listening to my story, making their verdict. Diagnosis: moderate clinical depression. Based on past efficacy, patient to continue with antidepressant medication. Dose to be maintained.

I went through periods of accidentally-on-purpose forgetting to take the pills for days, hoping I'd find they were nothing but placebo. One day I was standing in the fitting rooms of a clothes store, the light a little too harsh but the mirrors angled to make my reflection flattering. I noticed a dust mouse in the corner. A zap crackled though my head, like a strong electrostatic discharge in my skull. I thought I was having a stroke. Dizziness, nausea, confusion and these strange sensations in the brain are common when going cold turkey on SSRIs, so I'd have to restart the meds, before trying consciously or subconsciously to do without again.

How could I not keep on trying to quit, being told of innumerable ways of beating anxiety and depression without meds, how meds make you numb, that they are only a stopgap, a crutch, that you should exercise and mediate to make yourself feel better. That being in nature will heal your depression and cutting coffee will stop your anxiety. That psychiatric medication is unnatural but St John's wort and cod-liver oil are natural. That natural heals because natural is normal, and your mind is not. Nature is balance and your mind is un-. Be mindful. Accept. Let things pass, like clouds across the sky.

I float on the surface of a lake, my face turned to the sun, my body held by the darkness of the water below. In the periphery of my vision are pine trees and birches, the granite slabs of the shore, and just below, the edges of an aquatic meadow of waterlily leaves. My father taught me to swim in a lake like this. He held me up as I tried the strokes with my arms and legs, mimicking what I had seen him do with such ease. He held me up, and I thought I was swimming. He held me up, and I was swimming.

He held me up.

And then, he let go.

I didn't have time to close my eyes before I dipped beneath the surface, the glitter of summer sunshine replaced by underwater murk. Silence and the sway of thin green stalks. A stripy fish swam by, added by my imagination over the years.

The forced swimming test was seen as providing pharmacological evidence that learned helplessness is related to depression. However, while feeling a lack of control in aversive situations is a recognised component of depression, the learned helplessness theory of depression fails to explain variation in the aetiology and pathology of depression between individuals and situations. Nevertheless, the forced swimming test has been seen as a highly effective method to determine which drugs make it to clinical trials and was widely used in the development of selective serotonin reuptake inhibitors, famously Prozac, in the eighties.

Of course, I've had talking therapies. The first decade or so of my adult life I took what I could get on the National Health Service in the UK: six weeks of counselling, group CBT, individual CBT which I quit after the therapist cancelled a session by telling me she'd had a miscarriage, and six weeks of psychodynamic therapy. I gained some useful insights and tools and terminology to deal with and describe what was happening to me, because it kept happening. When I fell apart after my first dog died, I got a private therapist. I have been in therapy for most of the time since—another decade or so.

My first therapist lived in a very messy house. I thought maybe she had her priorities right, letting go of the small worry of tidiness. I told my first therapist how I struggled with the meaning of life in the face of death. That I seemed unable to shake the sense that whatever I did was meaningless, and thus I couldn't fully engage with anything. That since finishing my PhD I had stalled, intellectually and creatively.

My first therapist told me about accepting fallow periods. She told me that the absence of meaning in life is liberating because nothing matters. That mindfulness would allow me to ride the waves of my feelings. A lot of the time I bought it. It feels better when you can talk to someone about those feelings for an hour a week. You can park your emotions for Thursday at 11am and get on with your life.

I started writing my first novel, and I wrote this:

For a year and a half my therapist tried to persuade me that believing life has no meaning is a liberation, a way to freedom and fulfilment, to self-sufficient happiness and an easy being in the world. But she is wrong. It is a curse. What perversion of matter and time engenders a creature that is sentient of the obscene futility of its existence? What accident of chemistry combines into an organism that understands its utter lack of consequence?

I cut it out of the second draft of the novel.

I thought I was special. I thought that my pain set me apart. I thought there was a payoff, a prize. That's what I had been led to believe: that I was bullied not because I was weird but because I was gifted. I tried one thing and another in my adult life—working in an office, getting postgraduate degrees, teaching English language, becoming an academic, teaching English literature, writing academically, writing creatively, writing autobiographically. I was trying to find that prize, but the pain kept getting in the way. The more I failed to be the person I thought I should be, the more it hurt. The more it hurt the less I was able to be who I wanted to be.

On a regular basis I crumple to the floor and cry. I cry for a minute, for five, for twenty. I drag myself to bed and sleep. Then I get up and carry on. I swim on, despite the overwhelming feeling that my life has no meaning. There is nothing else to do. It is exhausting.

Of course, I've tried exercising. In my thirties, I started working out, and then I worked out some more. I became lithe and strong like I had never been before. Intense sessions lifting heavy things at the gym gave me a high. Was it the endorphins or the sense of control that made exercise seem like happiness?

Then I crashed. Cycles of exhaustion that masked as injuries.

My back hurt so much after my father died, and when my second dog was ill. Was it a bulging disc or grief? The two are hard to tell apart when you wake up each night to lift your paralysed dog. I can deadlift much more than a thirty-kilo dog. My trainer said, never grieve and lift, but I wanted the rush of my strength to mask the pain.

My second therapist had so many plants they spilled over from her windowsills onto the floor and crept towards the couch. I told my second therapist that although I had managed to move on from academic writing to the kind of writing I aways thought I wanted to do, it was still so damn hard. That I still didn't understand why I was alive. That I was still so very scared of dying. That I wanted to live forever but couldn't get out of bed.

My second therapist told me I needed to find my authentic self, my passion. Then things would feel easier, they would just flow. I started questioning whether writing was what I wanted to do. Every morning, I had to force myself to sit down and write. I gave myself the goal of five hundred words a day. I rarely managed to keep it up. Everything, including the most mundane household chores seemed easier than writing. Everything, including the most mundane household chores were tiring. I just wanted to sleep.

But some days I wrote five hundred words, and then I wrote five hundred more. And it felt like THIS. THIS wasn't my vocation or passion or authentic self or what I was put on this earth to do, but it was ecstasy. I couldn't tell you if it is something in my genes, or the way my brain is wired, or simply because I was brought up to value books and art above all else, but THIS is what I wanted to do. It was just so damn hard. So, I sat on my therapist's couch, and I thought that maybe I was wrong. That I should just do something else.

Of course, I've tried meditating. Sometimes it brought peace, many times it brought vivid images of the grossest violations that humans commit on other humans. I sat face to face with my existential angst and my behavioural despair. I sat. I sat. I sat. It felt like drowning.

My second therapist suggested that perhaps by taking antidepressants for over twenty years I had somehow broken my brain, made it unable to produce sufficient serotonin on its own. She encouraged me to stop. As I tapered down the meds, she kept telling me that I was talking and behaving and feeling the same. I wasn't. My thoughts started running away from me, I began obsessing over inconsequential things, like how to best explain to the builders renovating my study that they had put together the shelves wrong. For days I couldn't work or sleep, agonising over a conversation that would take three minutes. It was exhausting.

I was confused by my therapist's insistence: either the meds had an effect or not; either my brain was broken, or it was not. Maybe I didn't articulate my feelings well enough, or maybe she tried to normalise my anxiety. Perhaps she would have succeeded, if it wasn't for life happening.

My mother attempted suicide. For her, the meds stopped working. Her anxiety was so unbearable she did not want to live anymore. And when I was then hit by the most debilitating anxiety I have felt in my life—that anxiety that feels like dying without end—I was convinced our family was cursed by a hereditary disease, and I too was heading for a time when the pills would no longer keep me sane.

My father had died of cancer a few years prior. Although he claimed not to fear death when diagnosed, his last days were not calm. The metastases in his brain may have been to blame; when o longer knew where he was, or who we were, he still knew that something was terribly wrong. He tried to flee, to fight, to survive. No drugs worked, only full anaesthetic sedation. He died anaesthetised.

It is said that when you get stung by tentacles the deadly Irukandji jellyfish the delayed cardiac arrest is preceded by a sense of doom. Fear in its most pure form: the sense of impending death. Which is worse, the fear of death or the anxiety that feels like dying without end? Which one lies in store for me when the time comes?

I tried so hard, then, not to go back to the antidepressants. My second therapist said living through this crisis would make me understand I could survive without meds. The day I got home from the intensive care ward where my mother was recovering after her second overdose, I took half a Valium to sleep. My therapist was extremely disappointed. What should I have done instead? She suggested spraying my pillow with lavender scent. That's when I started thinking that perhaps she had never experienced what I was telling her about. That perhaps some people feel the unendurable pain of existence in ways unimaginable to others.

Sometimes life feels like swimming in a water-filled cylinder, sometimes like floating on a beautiful lake, but for some reason, staying above water seems like more of an effort for some of us, maybe because we're aware you can drown in both.

I told my third therapist about my mother. I told her I am no longer just scared of dying but also of living with an anxiety that is impossible to survive.

My third therapist told me that in some situations, whatever I do, I will feel bad. She told me that I will never stop being afraid of death. She told me its ok if I need to take some pills to survive. She told me I will never know why I'm here and what I'm doing, but that's ok, because I have already done so much. I didn't believe that last bit, but the rest made more sense than a lot of things I'd been told before.

My first novel, five years after being finished and after a redraft, finds a publisher. I also find an agent. Someone pays money, a small amount, but real money, into my account for a thing I wrote. I am a writer.

I always thought my exhaustion was depression, but when I kept hitting a wall with my physical exercise, I started to think that maybe there was more to it—and yet, I could do so much, lift so heavy, so how could my body be ill? Several false starts and years later I did get diagnosed with chronic fatigue syndrome/myalgic encephalomyelitis. My GP told me that, anecdotally, an SNRI has had good effect in CFS/ME patients. The diagnosing doctor thought it would make no difference, but my new psychiatrist agreed it was worth a try. Slowly I introduced an SNRI into my system after twenty-five years on SSRIs. SSRIs selectively inhibit only serotonin reuptake. SNRIs selectively inhibit both serotonin and norepinephrine reuptake.

The time coded as "immobility" in the forced swimming test has been shown to be reduced by a variety of antidepressant drugs, but their effect is not uniform. Antidepressants that selectively inhibit serotonin reuptake reduce immobility and increase swimming, while those that selectively inhibit norepinephrine reduce immobility and increase thrashing.

Within weeks of starting the new meds I had more energy, I felt more positive about life, and I was writing more. A lot more. But then, I also had a book a deal, and the recognition that a literary agent brings. I had finally been externally validated, that fallow period was perhaps coming to an end. Or perhaps writing was my passion, I just didn't know it. Maybe what one is meant to be doing is not an epiphany and passion, but part agonising decision and part painful perseverance. A lot of swimming.

Maybe a lifetime of living with and learning from anxiety and depression was coming to fruition. Maybe stepping back from excessive exercise redirected energy to my brain, the CFS/ME diagnosis allowing me to rest without guilt. Or maybe I have been on the most popular kind of antidepressant in the world my whole adult life, and all it has done is to make me swim. And swim. And swim. Round in circles. Getting nowhere.

Fig. 1. Rat showing typical posture of immobility after 10 min immersion in water.

I can't shake the image of a rat in a glass cylinder that accompanies the 1978 article by Porsolt et al. in the *European Journal of Pharmacology*, volume 47, that I read when I was trying to understand the difference between the drugs I have been taking: "Behavioural Despair in Rats: A New Model Sensitive to Antidepressant Treatments." I read the article, and it struck me like a bolt, like a brain zap: have the SSRIs made me sedately swim, when I could have been climbing and thrashing and knocking on the glass walls with my words?

But then I realise it is a false dichotomy because the choice is not between swimming or thrashing, but between swimming, thrashing, or giving in to the behavioural despair that means exhaustion and death. We don't speak about that last choice; Porsolt et al. never mention how many rats drowned in their experiments. Trying to escape the inescapable is tiring, thrashing means you reach exhaustion faster. I can't regret staying alive and staying alive without such pain that I could do nothing but despair. You can't write if you're drowning.

Maybe it is the black and white of the rat photograph, but I am reminded of Charlie Chaplin at the beginning of *Modern Times*. I think of rats swimming and workers in a factory, uncomplainingly performing repetitive tasks, except Chaplin's Tramp, for whom it all becomes too much. "He's crazy!" The title card screams. His bolt-tightening becomes a manic dance trashing the factory, as he thrashes against the giant machine. We all know how it must end—the Tramp is taken away in the back of an ambulance to be "cured of a nervous breakdown." Cured, so he can have another go at swimming in circles in modern times, in a world where he can neither sink nor swim.

Three Out of Four Ferrets
A Coda to Forced Swimming Test

LAKE Como is shaped like an upside-down Y and the western leg, lined with picturesque towns and luxury villas, is where the tourists go. George Clooney has a house there. I lived on the eastern leg, the non-Clooney side, for about a year. This side of the lake is also picturesque, but here the mountains rise steeply from the lake shore, so there is no room for luxury villas. I taught English in Lecco, where few tourists go, a small town home to small businesses including a small chocolate factory that made the air smell delicious if the wind was right. It's a wealthy but boring town. I used to escape to Milan, 45 minutes away by train, because I missed London more than I had expected. I missed the noise and buzz of a big city. Which is ironic, because it was in Lecco, a by Italian standards very quiet town, that I realised that I spoke like an Italian: too loud.

Scientists have proposed that there are numerous genes that increase the probability of an individual displaying traits of autism spectrum disorder (ASD) and attention-deficit/hyperactivity disorder (ADHD). Often these genes are linked to neurochemical functions that appear to be behind certain behavioural differences. For example, mutations in the FOXP2 gene have been connected to an alteration in the function of the neurotransmitter GABA which in turn changes the excitation/ inhibition balance. The inability to regulate activity and inactivity is something commonly associated with neurodevelopmental disorders, or so-called neurodivergence.

I'd taken a certificate in teaching English as a second language in a panic, trying to find a way out of my job in London after working in an office for three years. I was an account manager in sales and distribution at a magazine publishing house. That's the only time I have had a 9-5 office job, and I hated it. There were many reasons, but I think the main issue was being in an environment where what I was good at was encouraged and appreciated, but only within very narrow parameters.

"You can't fault her presentation skills," I overheard my boss tell his boss, after I had talked them through a sales report. The same skills that made me good at presentations, got me in trouble at other times: my directness, my voice. What was praised as clarity and confidence in a presentation, was interpreted as loud and rude when I sat at my desk.

Zebrafish larvae with the FOXP2 gene disabled swim further and faster than so-called wild-type zebrafish—those with the average genetic makeup found in the "wild." When these mutant zebrafish larvae were exposed to a solution of chemicals that increases GABA in the brain, such as methylphenidate (also known as Ritalin), their excessive locomotor activity decreased.

It also appears that the FOXP2 gene is responsible for vocal

motor control in animals that can make sounds. Studies show that
FOXP2 gene mutations—rather than deletion—disrupt song learning
in juvenile male zebra finches (not related to the zebrafish) and affect
language acquisition in humans and other mammals. The sounds
mice with these mutations make differ in number, frequency and
rhythm from wild-type mouse vocalisations.

My colleagues, in an effort to be kind and to suggest that I didn't
mean to sound as "abrupt" as I did, said it was because I was foreign.
I used to bristle at this. The way I communicated wasn't because
I was foreign, it was because I was *me*. I didn't understand why
being direct at work was a problem, or why talking at a level which
I didn't perceive as loud was an issue. This was who I was. But I was
given the foreignness excuse so many times by others that I started
to think there was something in it. Then, in one evening class for
the teaching certificate, we talked about conversation patterns in
different languages.

If you think about it, it's obvious. Conversations in different
languages sound different. Not just the words but the pitch, volume
and rhythm. It's a cultural thing. The Japanese leave gaps between
the end of one person saying something and the beginning of another
one speaking. It sounds deferent and hesitant to western ears. The
Italians, on the other hand, talk over each other, often raising their
voices—probably because they all talk at once, while the Japanese
can speak softly, one at a time. If a Japanese conversation, with a line

Speaker 1   ———————   ———————
Speaker 2   ———————   ———————

representing someone speaking, would look like this,

Speaker 1   ———————   ———————————
Speaker 2   ———————————   ———————

an Italian one would look like this,

Italian conversations often sound like arguments to Brits. God only knows how the Japanese interpret them. I once had an animated discussion about politics with an Italian friend in a restaurant in London, and our companions looked aghast. They thought we would come to blows any minute, whereas we were both on the same page: we'd gesticulate and bluster to show our distaste for the other's opinions, but at no point was it a personal matter. Not long after, we said goodbye with smiles and kisses.

So, was my loud voice culturally determined or is it part of my personality? Or do I sound the way I sound because of the way my brain is wired? When I was diagnosed with ADHD in my mid-forties, I was suddenly told that things that I thought were "just me" were actually a "disorder." Does that mean that some neurodivergent traits are seen as more or less divergent, or maybe not a disorder at all, in certain cultures, while other cultures pinpoint different characteristics as outside the norm?

Besides, I was quiet as a child.

Since the sounds mice make in the first few weeks of life are specific to their genetic strain, changes to early mouse vocalisations are considered a sign of an altered neurodevelopment due to genetic makeup. Some studies have shown that a lower rate of vocalisation in rodent pups is an indicator for ASD-type behaviour in adulthood, and thus the characteristic is often included in mouse models of autism. The same FOXP2 mutation which leads to fewer vocalisations in mouse pups, has been observed in human patients with ASD and delayed development of speech. ADHD, on the other hand, is associated with a lack of vocal inhibition, for example difficulty in waiting a turn in conversation or the inability to modulate speech volume.

I started writing "Forced Swimming Test" in a period of unusual mental energy. The new anti-depressant I was taking, a selective norepinephrine reuptake inhibitor or SNRI, seemed to make me happier, more forward-looking and more creative than I had been in a long time. In retrospect, I was in a hypomanic state. The hypo means that I was manic but in such a way that I could still function socially and professionally. In fact, I felt like I hadn't functioned so well socially or professionally for a long time, probably ever. It was exhilarating. I made a lot of new friends, and I wrote and wrote, and I started projects, and I packed my social media feeds with content. However, I was also aware that I was more impatient, impulsive and anxious. At times I felt on the edge of acting in ways I wasn't sure would be good for me, but often I felt compelled to do, to say, to write. To write. It was glorious to feel the ease with which I could write, my mind a well full of ideas and thoughts. A swirling, churning, chaotic kind of well.

This all complicated my relationship as a writer to psychiatric diagnoses and medication, and made me write "Forced Swimming Test." It seemed to me that antidepressants are deemed successful if they dull the terror and trauma of a drowning animal. They allow us to carry on swimming alongside our existential dread and numb us to the urge to escape our inescapable container. For me, escape—or at least attempts at escape—is trying to create meaning in an ultimately meaningless existence. After finishing that essay, I was diagnosed with ADHD, and changed my meds again, adding further complexity to my feelings around mental health, medication and creativity.

As I brusquely became aware when my mother attempted suicide, public mental health services in many, maybe most, countries struggle with funding for basic facilities, let alone identifying and addressing the individual needs of patients. Mental health services have become machines enabling patients to "function" and if that fails, to prevent suicides. Getting specialist mental health treatment is incredibly difficult and is often only offered after repeated mental health crises. Go to your GP with symptoms of depression and anxiety and they will start you on the first in a list of antidepressants licenced by NICE, and if the initial choice fails to help, work you down the list. Increasingly common is a referral for cognitive behavioural therapy, most likely in a generic form in a group on zoom.

Keep swimming.

Of course, for many this is sufficient, even helpful, at least in the short term. For those for whom it is not, lies a long line of trial and error with a number of medications, most often prescribed by a general practitioner who is short on time and expertise, and eventually a referral to secondary services, or rather, to the waiting list for such. In reality, people experiencing severe mental illness or a mental health crisis usually end up in A&E, some before they have had chance to harm themselves, some after. The quickest way to see a consultant psychiatrist on the NHS is to attempt suicide.

I am aware that I am very privileged to be able to afford private help when I have found myself in crisis, as I did after my mother's suicide attempts. I have now come to understand that the profound and overwhelming anxiety I ended up feeling after my mother's suicide attempts was an, albeit relatively mild, post-traumatic stress response. I experienced how being "triggered" is emphatically not simply being uncomfortable around a certain subject. Mentions of suicide and psychiatric institutions activated flashbacks in me that were accompanied by a surge in anxiety, sometimes panic, during a time when I was almost always feeling anxiety close to panic. I spent those weeks and months in a state of incredibly high alertness, to the point of not functioning.

Pain, stress and anxiety is associated with a neurotransmitter called Substance P. When released Substance P binds with NK1 receptors in the brain, which generate a range of neurochemicals, including dopamine and GABA, which in turn inhibit the excitatory responses evoked by Substance P.

Guinea pigs injected with compounds that stimulate Substance P make pronounced and long-lasting sounds, similar to those emitted by guinea pig pups separated from their mother. In one study, administering the antidepressant drugs imipramine or fluoxetine helped quieten the animals. This effect was seen in both the guinea pigs whose stress vocalisations were induced by injection and those in which they were caused by separation.

It was with some sense of failure that I restarted the SSRI medication I had quit some months previously. I was desperate to find relief. All I wanted, then, was to be able to function. Apart from the antidepressants, which do not have an immediate effect on anxiety or PTSD, the best my GP could do was beta-blockers (which suppress some of the physical manifestations of anxiety, such as a raised heart rate). Benzodiazepines are no longer prescribed by frontline services. Rightly so, as benzos frequently lead to worse mental health in the long run, but simply stripping these drugs out leaves a large hole in the provision of relief to people in crisis. We come back to the issue of waiting times. Most mental health referrals fall under the NHS commitment of an 18-week wait for non-urgent conditions. That's the aim, not the reality. I could not even have imagined waiting 18 weeks back then.

Having returned to the antidepressants I'd been taking on and off all my adult life, I wanted to know more about the implications of long-term use, and consider alternatives, with someone that specialised in the field. Although I had by then seen three different therapists, they were all more or less of the opinion that medication was a temporary solution, if not out-right harmful. I wanted to hear the other side of the story. Hoping to get some kind of balanced view, I chose a psychiatrist that came recommended and that I was told stressed the importance of talking therapies and other modalities. Still, I had the sense that I was somehow talking to the enemy, to someone who would prescribe me happy pills with a share in the profits, without a care for the damage they were doing to my brain.

The same study into Substance P also found that administering a new compound being developed by pharmaceutical company Merck, MK-869, had the same effect as other antidepressants in quieting the guinea pig pups. This new compound worked specifically on NK1 receptors and was seen as a possible new lucrative drug to treat affective disorders. However, a clinical trial in humans failed to show that MK-869 outperformed placebo and in 1999 Merck announced that the drug would be shelved as an antidepressant. The price of Merck shares fell by 5%. Later Merck announced that the drug might find a limited market as a treatment for nausea during chemotherapy, when a study in 2000 found that "MK–869 prevented retching and vomiting in three out of four ferrets."

My first psychiatrist dispelled some of my unease. She considered all aspects of my life and put a great deal of thought into what approach to take to medication, clearly explaining her rationale. She held off changing my treatment for a year until she got to know me. Since SNRIs are associated with more side-effects and are harder to quit than SSRIs she was reluctant to change me onto this type of drug, but in the light of my CFS/ME diagnosis she agreed it would be useful to try it, with a view of tapering the medication I was already on if it worked well. Cue the markedly higher mood about two weeks after starting the new drug.

It was while I was writing "The Forced Swimming" test that I emailed my psychiatrist the following: "I have recently realised that a lot of my issues are similar to those of people with ADHD," here I listed a range of symptoms that fitted a textbook ADHD diagnosis. I then added, "I don't mean to imply that I necessarily have ADHD, I just wanted to explore if this observation may help us."

I had been becoming increasingly aware of what being neurodivergent meant, partly because of the increased discussion around the topic generally, and by meeting—in real life and online—people that had been diagnosed or self-identified as neurodivergent. I didn't think *I* could be neurodivergent, however. I am old enough to have a rooted image of what autism and ADHD look like, and it is male, teenage and maladjusted. I was a quiet child, performing well in school, and a "highly-functioning" adult, performing well in academia. I wondered if the SNRIs were somehow causing the ADHD-like symptoms.

While dopamine was previously believed to be central to ADHD, it is now accepted that such a multifaceted disorder involves more than a single neurotransmitter system. In humans, alteration in the function of GABA has also been linked with ADHD, as has the dysregulation of serotonin, norepinephrine, glutamate, and histamine. These chemicals allow the cortex region of the brain, associated with conscious decisions and actions, to modulate the processes of the subcortex, which is related to non-conscious processes. This unconscious activity in the subcortex has been found to have a central role in emotional and social functions in humans.

By the time that my first psychiatrist referred me for assessment for ADHD and autism at a specialist clinic, I had changed medication again. I didn't want to lose the high that the SNRI gave me, but it also came with side effects I couldn't tolerate. We decided to try bupropion, a norepinephrine-dopamine reuptake inhibitor, instead. Commonly prescribed for depression in North America, bupropion comes with fewer side effects than both SNRIs and SSRIs. I presume cost is the reason that it is only very rarely prescribed in the UK, and only by consultant psychiatrists—it is not on the list that GPs follow. It has worked very well for me, however, which makes some sense in retrospect. Bupropion is one of the few antidepressants that acts on dopamine.

The five-choice serial-reaction time task (5CSRTT) is used to test the attention and impulsivity of laboratory animals. In one study, following learning the 5CRTT, "standard" lab rats were decapitated and brain pieces analysed for levels of dopamine, serotonin and other neurochemicals. A higher level of dopamine was found to improve choice accuracy, which fits with pharmacological studies showing that methylphenidate, which boosts dopamine, increases focus.

However, a high level of serotonin appeared to impair choice accuracy in the rats. The lack of serotonin is typically associated with low mood, but serotonin is also connected with a wide range of other functions in the brain, such as learning, memory, and reward mechanisms, as well as in the rest of the body, including pain, digestion and nausea, sleep, thermoregulation, sexual activity and even healing and bone density.

I was assessed for both ADHD and autism, a process that was useful and bizarre in equal measure. My second psychiatrist, the doctor leading this evaluation, was open about the arbitrariness and crudeness of the methods available to her. She stressed that being neurodivergent and receiving a diagnosis of neurodivergence is not the same thing. The threshold of a medical diagnosis of ADHD or autism (or other "disorders" now considered manifestations of neurodivergence), is that the condition significancy impairs daily life. Hence, her description of me as having "ADHD with autistic traits"—the latter do not hinder me sufficiently in my life to warrant a diagnosis of autism.

I am someone who feels like an impostor with every diagnosis, so on the one hand I can't but wonder to what extent my ADHD has ever held me back in life when I have been able to achieve most things I have put my mind to. On the other hand, the diagnosis did provide a new context for some of the difficulties I have been experiencing all my life, and gave an explanation for many of my behaviours that have been seen (often by myself) as undesirable, or unappealing. However, it also categorised some of my traits and skills that I had seen as useful and even exceptional, as manifestations of a "disorder." Thus, my diagnosis was both validating and invalidating, accompanied by a sense of relief (it's not my fault) and a sense of insufficiency (I'm not normal).

Genetically altered mice which lack the NK1 receptor that moderates the stress response evoked by Substance P are generally hyperactive and show deficits in attentional processing. Compared to other mice, they make an increased number of omission errors and premature responses as they work through the 5CRTT, suggesting that under increased attentional demand these genetically modified mice are both inattentive and impulsive. Therefore, mice with the NK1 receptor gene knocked out are seen as a good model for ADHD. When NK1 deficient mice received amphetamine or methylphenidate, hyperactivity and attention returned to the level of saline-treated wild-type mice.

Most importantly, for me, the diagnosis has allowed me to reconceptualise some of the mental distress I have felt in my life, not as an illness but as a response. I am anxious and depressed, not because I have generalised anxiety disorder or depression, but because my brain does not function well in many situations that are common and even essential to everyday life as most of us are expected, and to a certain extent forced, to live it. My brain has a hard time filtering and ordering, which means it gets inundated by too much input or information, whether that is wandering the isles of a supermarket or facing a workweek ahead—both situations that make me overwhelmed to the extent that I feel paralysed, unable to choose the kind of rice I want, or begin any of the simple tasks I need to get on with in the day. The energy I have to expend to overcome that paralysis, at least to the extent that I can survive and function as an adult, leads to fatigue and eventually depression. Being diagnosed with ADHD has made me feel less like a failure to have lived a life where I have avoided a "normal" 9-5 work—especially in an office—a life I have organised so that I can incorporate the "excessive" rest I need. Where my hyperfocus, when it hits, is an asset. And a loud voice is great when you are lecturing.

Because some neurodivergent traits are very useful indeed in this world where sociability, productivity and profit are the measures of success. I am very good at learning and making connections between ideas, so I'm a great academic. As a child I tended to hyperlexia (as opposed to dyslexia), learning to read on my own very early on, and I had a near photographic memory when I was at school. This made tests easy: I simply recalled the relevant page and paragraph of my textbooks. My particular brand of neurodivergent brain was very well suited to school, where reading and learning was my main goal, ordered and set out for me in a strict schedule. I wasn't a sociable child, so I had few distractions. I *was* different, but in a way that was seen as sign of success, not a hindrance.

The difficulties came when my life started involving more—

of everything. More daily tasks, more choices, more socialising. Confronted with all this input, the brain that had functioned so well in a limited, controlled environment, started to falter. I now understand that I was medicated to deal with all that. Or rather, it was the symptoms I was experiencing as a consequence of dealing with all that which were medicated. In the face of the apparently inescapable glass container of life, I needed help to keep on swimming.

My ADHD diagnosis and this reconceptualisation of my mental distress further complicated my relationship with medication. With the ADHD diagnosis I was given membership to a club where taking meds is ok, even encouraged. Nobody expects you meditate your neurodivergence away. On the one hand, it is a relief to be told medication can help without the imperative of a cure. On the other, the inevitable question is: if I am not mentally ill, why am I taking medication?

The genetically altered mouse most extensively used as a model for autism is the inbred BTBR strain. BTBR mice display abnormal sociability and repetitive behaviours. They leave fewer scent marks and make fewer sounds during social interactions, their calls are different from and less complex than those of wild-type mice, and they struggle with the social transmission of food preference that happens among other mice.

Genetically altered mice that display these kinds of autism-relevant behaviours have been injected with existing and experimental drugs in a number of studies. In some of the studies the drugs were shown to reduce the levels repetitive behaviour and increase time spent exploring and sniffing nose to nose with strange mice.

For example, wild-type mice given the choice of an empty cup and a cup with a mouse in it, prefer spending time by the cup with the mouse, while mice with the CNTNAP2 gene knocked out show no difference in preference between the cups. However, when treated with oxytocin, a hormone that stimulates social bonding, the mutant mice show a strong preference for interacting with the cup containing a mouse.

I am suspicious of the "trend" of increased neurodivergent diagnoses, not because I believe that people seek or are given diagnoses incorrectly, but because when something receives that much attention on mainstream and social media, it becomes an obvious way to make money for everyone from big pharma to makers of notebooks and earplugs, and the lived experience that drives people to seek a diagnosis becomes misunderstood and trivialised and even plain forgotten.

Even more problematically for me, that lived experience, which by definition is one that involves some kind of distress (or it wouldn't make people seek medical explanation or help), becomes pathologized. A diagnosis of neurodivergence is still a diagnosis of dysfunction, something to be set right—whether by medication or other interventions. But neurodivergence is not like cancer, that some of us get and others dodge, it's not curable or incurable, it won't (directly) kill you. Neurodivergent people are not ill, and I even hesitate to say that they are "different." Yes, and bear with me here, everyone is a little bit autistic.

Everyone has some kind of experience of the traits and symptoms associated with neurodivergence, but not everyone is neurodivergent. Neurodivergent people are not aliens, they experience the same things as all humans, but they experience these to a greater or lesser degree than is—and this is crucial—*acceptable* in what is considered a "normal life." I keep coming back to a simple but effective analogy that I can't claim to have invented: everyone needs to pee, but if you need to pee sixty times a day it is problematic.

So, while everyone is a little bit autistic insofar as they have had the experiences that autistic people have, say of feeling awkward in social situations, or being bothered by a loud noise, not everyone experiences these to such an extent that it makes "normal" life as we conceive of it difficult. Crucially, neurotypical experiences of anxiety and overwhelm can generally be thought away, aided by desensitisation or cognitive behavioural therapy, while neurodivergent experiences of the same generally cannot. Equally, everyone who is disorganised is "a little ADHD," but there's a difference between disorganisation which can be remedied by using a planner, and struggling to pay attention to and usefully prioritise tasks, which can't.

The SHR/NCrl strain of rats is seen as displaying the core characteristics of ADHD, including hyperactivity, inattention, and impulsivity. In one study, these mutant rats along with non-mutant ones got rewards for pressing illuminated levers. After a period, the reward scheme changed and treats were dispensed from levers in specific locations instead, regardless of illumination. Trial and error, accuracy and reaction time was measured. Some rats then received an electrical current to their brain, delivered through electrodes placed on the rats' shaved heads. While initially the SHR/NCrl rats performed worse than wild-type rats in the task, the ones which received electrical stimulation to their brain subsequently performed as well as the normal rats.

Apart from being told I was loud, another reason I found working in an office difficult is because I am generally contrary. I don't like authority, and I don't like being told what to do. Some say this is also part of my neurodivergent brain. I'd like to think there is more to it than that, because one of the things I don't like the most is a simplistic explanation or solution. The world is a complicated and often shitty place, and the reason it stays shitty is because solving complex problems is hard. The reason we don't have a cure for cancer is not because someone hasn't yet found—or is secretly withholding—the one simple remedy, but because it is a really difficult thing to cure. And so is mental illness, or rather, mental distress.

The idea that there is a straightforward way to fix mental distress drives me up the wall. And yet, all I want is a simple solution. I don't deny that I hope that the next pill will cure me the way that some people hope that an "all natural" diet or praying will. We will all be disappointed.

What really gets my goat is people telling me that taking St John's wort or meditating or exercising is somehow inherently better than taking antidepressants, as if all those things weren't ultimately working by way of the same mechanism: altering your mind. Nobody exists without altering their consciousness, whether that be by spraying lavender on their pillow and writing a gratitude journal, drinking coffee or smoking pot, taking headache pills (yes, they help you function better cognitively, too, it's hard to think with a headache) or antidepressants.

I do think that the fact that some remedies are sold for profit while others are freely available is problematic. What is more problematic to me, however, is the idea that we need any of these things, that we can and should be, if not cured, then changed. After all, the reason that people part with their hard-earned cash for any remedy, whether it be apple cider vinegar or methylphenidate, is that they want to get *better*. But better how? Better at what?

Mindfulness techniques affect neurotransmitter systems in the brain and have been associated with increased levels of serotonin. Individuals who regularly practice meditation have been found to have higher levels of GABA. Meditation has also been shown to increase rhythmic activity in the anterior cingulate cortex (ACC). The ACC is connected to both the cortex and the subcortex and is thought to be the place where outside stimuli and internal motivation are processed together. It is particularly involved in decision making.

In one study, the ACC in mice was rhythmically stimulated by light pulses via optic fibres implanted in the brain. The behaviour of the mice in a light/dark box was assessed pre-stimulation. Mice that tend to stay in the dark side of the box are seen as more anxious, those that explore the light side as less so. The mice then began once-daily 30-min pulsed-light sessions, 5 days a week, for 4 weeks. The behaviour of the mice was re-assessed at the end of each week. Treated mice showed increased exploratory behaviour in the light side of the box, indicating lower anxiety.

I dislike pandering to the past. Things were mainly not that much better before, or at least on the whole neither better nor worse. Each age has its share of suffering and pain. Before societies existed, life must have been pretty short and brutal. And society not only expects but necessitates conformity—it's by working together that we survive. But survival doesn't equal happiness. Somehow, at some time, the idea that we can and should be happy emerged. Perhaps it was with the move from a society in which authority and obedience was seen as necessary, and happiness for the vast majority was only conceived as possible in the next life, to a society in which individual agency and freedom was prized, that the possibility of making yourself happy emerged. Except, of course, the aim of both types of society, perhaps society itself at its very core, is not happiness but accumulation. The very idea of individually engendered happiness is not a purely metaphysical one, but inextricably linked to a world that prizes continued accumulation beyond any reasonable limits.

Humans are hoarders: like birds and beavers and racoons

that pile up tin cans we accumulate to survive. From hunting and gathering to the collection of personal data from social media users. It's just very hard for us to stop, it seems, when we have enough. Perhaps it is because we have no one to stop us, perhaps it is because we have come to believe that more is going to make us happy, and that we can all have more: more things, more happiness.

Capitalism is just a system society has evolved to maximise accumulation. Part of the success of capitalism is persuading people that accumulation can be done equally, that it is accessible to everyone, when, in fact, the best way to accumulate is to concentrate, maximising it for some and minimising for others. At least pre-capitalist systems didn't hide the fact that most people were left with fuck all. The lie of equity is a pretty substantial upgrade in the case for accumulation, however. People who think they work for themselves, work more. The sleight of hand of capitalism, making us believe we can all have a slice of the pie, achieves the double win of making people work more and be more amenable to work: because they believe they are working towards their own happiness.

It's not that capitalism makes some of us unhappy, although it patently does, it's that capitalism makes us believe that we can all be happy, and then happier. That is the very driving force of capitalist accumulation, in a world where for many, mere survival is no longer an issue. We could, should, have stopped accumulating a long time ago if simply surviving, even simply being comfortable and content, was our aim.

Yet another mutant mouse model of neurodivergence, DAT-KO mice—mice with the gene for a dopamine transporter knocked out, causing a dopamine deficiency—display behaviours associated with both autism and ADHD. DAT-KO mice are hyperactive, not inclined to socialise with new mice, more likely to engage in repetitive behaviours and less likely to get used to startling stimuli (such as loud noises). In two separate studies, DAT-KO and wild-type mice were assessed using the marble burying test. All mice were acclimatised to a cage filled with soft bedding and then removed from the cage for a short while. When returned, each mouse faced 15 marbles resting on top of the bedding in the cage, evenly spaced in a 3x5 configuration.

One set of scientists interpreted the results as caused by "severe hyperactivity and related attention deficit" in the DAT-KO mice. The other team speculated that the test showed "impaired action selection (the task of resolving conflicts between competing behavioural alternatives)" in the mutant mice. In both studies, the mice with a dopamine deficiency buried fewer marbles than other mice.

Mental distress, its pathologisation and its putative cures are intimately linked with the economic system we find ourselves living in. A system in which the majority have to live in a way that maximises accumulation for the few is not a way of life that suits everyone equally well. The generation of surplus value, a.k.a. a level of productivity that exceeds the producer's immediate needs, is better achieved in certain situations and with certain human traits, neither of which is immutable. To go back to the earlier analogy, in a world where piss is worth as much as gold, needing to pee sixty times a day would be considered productive rather than problematic.

If productivity is our benchmark for happiness, our yardstick for a successful life, or even just our template for a normal way of living, quite a few of us will never be happy. Not only because many of us do not have the traits required to live such a life, but because the idea that productivity, and ultimately accumulation, equals happiness is a false one. It is a glass cylinder filled with water.

My issue, then, with mental health and medication goes

further than an issue with big pharma and profits. Big pharma, as a cog in the machine, is not only there to make money by selling us sugar pills. The meds it sells us *work*: they help those who struggle to function, making society run smother, better, producing more. But so do most "alternative" remedies. So does the very idea that we should be "happy." So does the idea that certain other things, such as creativity, makes us happy. Often, the imperative to creativity, held up as an alternative to "work," is a thinly veiled encouragement of productivity. Often, the way we measure creativity is by the yardstick of productivity. Make art for art's sake. Make. Always make more.

What most mental health cures, pharmacological, natural, chemical, or otherwise, do is not make you happy, but make you *functional*. Functional means being economically active—accumulating—or if that is unachievable, being as small a drain on others' accumulated resources as possible. There's a difference between being functional and being happy. There is a difference between being happy and being free of mental distress. There is a difference between being functional, happy or without mental distress, and being who you are or want to be. These things are not the same. To me, medication as well as therapy serve the purpose to make me free of mental distress that I find unacceptably painful, such as crippling anxiety, so that I am able be who I want to be, or at the very least, explore who I want to be. However, as who I want to be is inevitably conditioned by the society I live in, I want to be someone who produces art. I like to think that this kind of productivity is somehow better, less complicit with the system, but I am not sure that is true.

What I do know is that while the idea of neurodivergence is useful to a great extent, it is also a gross simplification, a way to categorise difference that makes it easier to peddle cures, to tell those that are different how to best become same. How to keep swimming in their own lane.

An enriched environment has been shown to be disproportionately beneficial to rats lacking genes for producing serotonin. Animals that naturally produce serotonin seem unaffected by environmental manipulation. A mutation in the 5-HTT gene in humans leading to lower serotonin production seems to enhance vulnerability to develop depression after exposure to stressful events, such as a deterioration in living conditions.

I want to end this essay on a hopeful note, saying something like, "once we've diagnosed all the artists as ADHD and all the scientists as autistic, please can we just go back to agreeing that human brains are amazing and diverse." I want to suggest that rather than pathologising some types of brains or calling them dysfunctional or disordered, and medicating them to fit in, maybe we could just recognise that we don't all want and need the same things to thrive, and adapt our expectations of what a normal life looks like, making allowances for people to exist differently, recognising that success comes in different shapes.

But even though the lanes of this circular swimming pool that we find ourselves in may be broadened, I don't believe that it is possible to escape it. Instead, I think it is time to acknowledge that we will not be happy—almost certainly not most of the time, perhaps not even some of the time. Being happy is not the aim of life. Take that burden off your shoulders. The aim of life is to survive. Do what you need to do to survive.

If you are too loud, or too quiet, the real challenge is not to fit in. It's not even to be content with not fitting in. It is to be upset about not fitting in. It is to find a way to be upset about not fitting in, about trying to fit in and failing, about deciding to be different and failing at that too. And feeling all of it. Feeling the inescapability of feelings. Don't swim quietly but scrabble against the glass cylinder, vocalise—or don't. Get things wrong, take your time choosing and be impatient, bury fewer marbles. Be sensitive. Bite.

"Signs of hyperactivity/impulsivity include difficulty in maintaining stillness, excessive vocalization, constant movement, persistent attention-seeking and play, prompt reaction or anticipation to events, impatience with waiting, less than eight hours of sleep a day and poorer sleep quality, intolerance to delayed reward, excessive object destruction, lack of self-control (such as uninhibited biting), hypersensitivity (reaction to stimuli that are permanently present in the environment), lack of food satiety, and communication difficulties with other dogs and humans."

Emotional Dysregulation

MY dad and I used to dye Easter eggs on Maundy Thursday, getting them ready to put into baskets with bread and salt and other food. My mother and I would take them to church to be blessed during mass on the Saturday before Easter Sunday, as is the Polish Catholic tradition. My dad didn't go to church. The egg dye came in small tablets that we dissolved in boiling water and a little vinegar, in tall old Nescafé jars. There were five colours: green, blue, yellow, red and violet. Then we carefully lowered the eggs, hard boiled already, into the dye and let them sit. You had to stir them gently so that they wouldn't end up with white spots where they rested against the glass at the bottom or sides of the jars. I was always impatient to get the eggs out, but if you fished them out too early, they ended up pale. Left long enough the shells took on deep and brilliant colours, which we made shine by rubbing the eggs in cooking oil.

In my first novel I wrote: *Her dad is dying. And she is the one to break the news to him. That Tuesday afternoon she tells her father he has metastatic lung cancer.* Her was my, she was I. Every time I write I find myself writing about my father's death, and then I think, that's so banal, enough already. He was sick, he died. Watching your father die happens to so many people, I'm not special. They don't all go on about it.

But maybe they should.

My fourth therapist said in an introductory phone call, "you've probably been told you're too sensitive a lot in your life." I burst into tears. I was looking for a new therapist after my ADHD diagnosis. The one I found specialises in late diagnosed women, being one herself. She's helped me unwind a lot of the terms I have used about myself for years, pathologizing, minimising and devaluing my own experiences, especially with regard to feelings: "too sensitive," "overanxious," "neurotic," and now "emotionally dysregulated." Emotional dysregulation is seen as a common trait with ADHD, but my fourth therapist always asks, what does the "dys" mean? What would emotional *regulation* look like?

I was surprised at how many friends and acquaintances, after an initial, "sorry to hear about your dad," never mentioned his passing again. Never asked how I was. It was given I was grieving, but I was meant to grieve privately. One of the hardest things when you have lost someone, as Auden well knew, is the way the world seems to go right on, and you are expected to go on with it. We have lost our mourning traditions, some with good reason, but I wish we had something to symbolise our emotional state after the death of a loved one. To guide us when we are at a loss.

My friend's father passed a few years ago, and my friend performed a range of traditional Hindu rituals throughout an intense ten-day mourning period, including shaving his hair. I remember being envious. It would have been a relief to have a script of rituals, whatever they may be, to follow when my father died. Be given a period in which one is allowed to grieve openly, in which one has company in grief and ways of showing one's grief. The shaving of the hair especially appeals to me, in the way it signals dramatic loss and the process of coming to terms with grief slowly. My mother wore a small black rosette after her mother died. She didn't after my father passed away.

I remember dad and I waiting for my mum to come home. It is probably very close to five pm, because I am very anxious in this memory. I am anxious because I am sure something has happened to my mother.

On most days I was ok during the day but about half an hour before either of my parents were due home, panic started rising in me. I tried to play or read or watch TV but as it got closer to the time of them arriving it became harder and harder to distract myself from the churning inside. I couldn't help myself thinking, what if my dad has been in a car crash? What if my mum has fallen ill? What if she has been pushed on the train tracks? Something, anything, terrible could have happened. I used to pray to God to make it not so. I became fidgety, and eventually I wouldn't be able to sit still and I'd start pacing.

This particular afternoon I try not to show it to my dad, but he can see. "Are you anxious?" He asks. I remember the coffee table in the living room, and the rug on which it stood, and the pattern in red on the rug and then my puke on the pattern. In my memory my dad rushes up, stands over me, dabs some kitchen roll on the rug to get the stain out. He is angry. I can't remember if he says anything, but I can feel it in the way he stands. I am sorry.

It's ok to be upset if you have something to be upset about. Something to which your grief or anxiety or depression is proportional. If a loved one dies, it is ok to grieve, for some time, unobtrusively, but not for too long if the person is a parent or grandparent or more distant relative. More obvious and long-lasting grief is permitted if a spouse or child dies, but you shouldn't keep on mourning someone for too long (prolonged grief disorder).

It is ok to be a bit anxious before an exam, say, or a public speaking event—everyone is nervous about those—or when waiting for news of a loved one that's going under the knife, maybe, or the outcome of a life-changing decision. It is not ok to be anxious about things that you must do in everyday life, like shopping or going to work, and definitely not about cleaning (generalised anxiety disorder). It's not ok to be so depressed about a job that you can't go to work. It's not ok to be depressed about the meaninglessness of life or the fact that we are all going to die (clinical depression).

If you are anxious about things like flying, it is understandable because your brain is making a logical error and can be re-educated, unless, of course, it doesn't respond to desensitisation (hypersensitivity). It's very much not ok to be anxious when it comes to attachments to other people. Forming deep bonds to people is quite undesirable (anxious attachment). Taking criticism to heart and perceiving indifference or anger from someone without cause is no good at all (rejection sensitive dysphoria).

An anxious child is something that needs to be fixed. Children should not refuse to go to school. Children should not want to play alone all the time. Children should be happy and carefree and like playing with their friends. Although babies normally go through a period of separation anxiety, older children should not worry about their parents dying every time they go out of the house (separation anxiety disorder). Children should not be so anxious they throw up on the carpet.

Like so many of us I have repeatedly been told by therapists, including the fourth one, that I need to learn to "parent myself." However, the practicalities of how to achieve this parenting of the self have never been clearly explained to me. I understand the logic behind the idea that the best way to allay anxiety or other uncomfortable feelings as an adult is to provide yourself with the reassurance and guidance a parent would give to their child. I understand that ultimately, for this assurance to feel safe and available it needs to come from oneself rather than relying on others.

But I never knew how that would look in practice. How do I parent myself? Therapists would explain: the way you would soothe a child. But I have never soothed a child. And as a child I wasn't soothed—not the way I needed, anyway. In therapy I'd haltingly rehearse comforting phrases, suggest physical contact, voice ideas of allowing and holding space for emotions—in therapy I said I would do all those things to soothe my inner child, but I never really felt they would be effective. Because I had never felt them being effective.

My dad and I used to play a lot together when I was small. We often played a board game that I loved—I'm sure it has long since been cancelled—where the aim was to gather all the gemstones on a map of Africa. My dad and I played Ludo, we played Fish-in-the-Sea, and we played Memory. We played early video games together. Later my dad told me how dull he found these games (as an adult, I too find board-games very tedious) but he never showed that boredom to me as a child. My dad and I played again and again. Often, we played games as he tried to distract me from being anxious. It didn't work.

The reason one feels anxiety is no doubt often connected to the way one was—or wasn't—parented. The very idea of self-parenting rests on the premise that a parent is able to help with unpleasant or inappropriate emotions. But it's not an easy thing to do.

My mother would minister her medical skills, which would work as a comfort to me, but only if my distress was from a physical source. Because she found it hard to acknowledge purely emotional distress, at best she would try to argue with my logic: "no, nothing bad will happen, there are no monsters under the bed, I will come back from work every day." And part of me wondered for a long time, what else could I do for a scared child, but tell them the same lies? Because bad things do happen, people die—we die. In the end, my mother's way of allaying the fears she couldn't disprove was to medicate me.

My father understood this anxiety that cannot be argued or thought away, because he had felt it too, but I think this made him afraid of feelings. He struggled with seeing his child in distress, when he himself had no way of dealing with his own. Although I remember my father as very warm and loving, my main memory of his reaction to my deep anxiety, anxiety so bad that I threw up, was anger. I made him angry. Mopping up my sick from the carpet, he was angry.

I don't blame my parents for these each in their own way inappropriate reactions to my mental distress. They both wanted to help me, to allay my discomfort, to make it stop. For me and for them. They're not unusual, and very much products of a culture that discourages extreme emotions. And they were dealing with unresolved pain themselves. But it means that I, by definition, don't have any models for how to soothe an anxious child in the way that I need to be soothed. I don't think I'm alone in this. I have tried imagining how I would comfort my child self, but it has never felt like it was more than a thought experiment. Until an unexpected turn at the end of an unplanned recreational LSD trip.

I was home and I took a microdot of LSD. A microdot, I thought, won't do much, so I took another one. I started watching a film. It was a film about war, and although I was objectively aware that it most likely was meant to be bleak, at some point things on screen started to sparkle. Some scenes seemed set in the world of the old Windows start-up screen, with its gently rolling, intensely green grass hills and impossibly blue sky. Looking away from the TV screen I realised that it wasn't just the film—everything around me had a sheen and a glitter. At this stage there were no intense visualisations, just an inner and outer glow. I very much enjoyed the film, even though I was aware that my enjoyment had less to do with what I was watching than the trip I was on. I am always aware of the fact that I am tripping when I am on psychedelics, which makes me feel safe enough to embrace the ride.

That night, until I went to bed this high was just a pleasurable experience. Then, as I tried to go to sleep my mind started churning. It started to go through repeated cycles of intense emotions, from sadness, frustration and anger to a sense of relief, insight and joy. Initially these cycles revolved around issues and challenges in my present. When I opened my eyes, things dissolved into triangles. I mused on how when I take psilocybin, things appear swirly, while on LSD they become spiky.

My mind looping is nothing unusual, but the LSD made it more intense, the emotions more raw, and I was crying a lot. Famously, LSD was studied as a potential adjunct to therapy until it was outlawed in the late 1960s, and research has slowly recommenced in recent years. With this trip I really understood how LSD could work therapeutically. Rather than my thoughts being stuck in an unproductive, repetitive cycle in the present, the psychedelic added a dimension of depth to my ruminations: with each revolution my mind was going deeper into my mind, further back. The drug also loosened the boundaries of my ego. My present self was always very much there, but I also felt like I could inhabit past selves.

Time was losing its significance, both in the moment and in memory. I found myself with a hand on my brow, gently stroking my own head. I was holding myself as an infant. Holding a baby does not come naturally to me, I have rarely wished for a child and certainly do not now. This was not just a baby, this was me. And I became aware that, finally, I was parenting myself. Not simply as an idea or thought, but as an intense experience. I felt like I was able to soothe, and I felt soothed. But my mind, or perhaps more accurately now, my emotions, were still revolving, evolving. I faced my parents, the adult I and the child I together. I said to them, "don't be angry at me, please don't be angry that I am anxious." To myself, still holding and caressing the child me, I said, "you're just a child, you will be sad and scared, but you're safe. You're ok." This allowed me to turn to my parents again, to tell them, "don't be angry, I'm just a child." I remember this intensely, repeating "I'm just a child. Don't be angry, I'm just a child." At first, pleading, then increasingly as a statement, a confrontation.

Another memory, that is most likely a composite of memories: we are in the car, my mum, my dad, and I. I think we are going to a lake to swim. My dad is driving. I am in the back on a booster seat. My mother, in the front, is talking to my father. I want her to stop talking. She is saying things that are making my dad angry. But she won't stop. I think I try to say something to smooth things over. But whatever I say makes things worse. At one point my dad shouts that he's had enough. He turns the car around and we go home. We never made it to the lake that day.

I am aware I am narrativising now as I reflect on the LSD experience, but whether or not this is a convenient story dreamt up whilst on drugs, it seems to me that I was able confront my parents because the adult me was there for my child self. It felt like a therapeutic move towards recognising my parents' responsibility and letting go of some the guilt about being anxious as a child that has carried over as shame at being intensely emotional as an adult. Although I did feel a profound sense of calm for some days after this experience, I don't want to suggest that I was in some way "healed" by this trip. However, it did enable me to finally understand what self-parenting is and can achieve. Importantly, it made me feel allowed to feel. It didn't resolve or allay or cure my anxiety but made me accept that being anxious is part of me and that is ok.

The trip ended with a sense that I was no longer held by myself but by a collective or cosmic being. I had visions of being supported or held up by multiple women, then a kind of all-encompassing mother. I am aware how clichéd this sounds. I don't know if the drugs made me connect to some kind of existing entity, or simply made my brain release chemicals that made me feel this connection, or whether my narrative mind created an idea and feeling that I craved.

The main reason I have been experimenting with psychedelics in midlife is to find something that would make me less afraid of dying. I've always been afraid of death. Not of the pain and indignity that comes with dying, although that also worries me, having seen my father die. No, I feel panic rising when I think about the moment of death, becoming nothing, everything ending. Imagining myself not existing is almost unbearable for me. Being dead is inconceivable.

I hear people say how a long life would be awful, boring and tedious. To me, if I can stay healthy, it sounds great. One human lifetime is not enough, there is so much to do and know. To experience. I'd start with studying for all the university degrees and read all the books, in my own time, watching every sunset and sleeping deliciously and without remorse every afternoon. There would be time to take it slow and to live life to its fullest too.

There are only very few people I have met that feel the same, but when we find each other, it's a revelation. "Yes," we say to each other, "of course we wouldn't be bored!" Not for a very, very long time. We'd do all the things.

Am I too sensitive in fearing death intensely and frequently? Perhaps it's just that I think the thought through, of how it would be to die, when most people do not allow themselves to. Maybe my sensitivity lies in what I allow myself to perceive. Or what I cannot help perceiving, thinking, feeling. Studies have shown that neurodivergent brains tend to have more and different neural connections than "normal" brains. In newborns, human brains create an immense amount of new neural connections, and the process of infant learning is one of "pruning" and consolidating these connections—we gain skills by making efficient neural pathways, we learn to navigate the world by filtering out unimportant information. It would make sense that brains with a wealth, maybe a surfeit, of neural connections and a lack of distinct pathways would produce intense emotions, generate new ideas and make unusual links, but also get easily overstimulated and overwhelmed.

Another game my dad and I used to play was one where you had to construct ants out of different body parts in colourful plastic. The aim was to create an ant all in one colour, but I remember the ants turning out with orange bodies and purple legs and green heads.

The hardest part of watching my father die was seeing how after he had said he wasn't afraid to die, his last days of consciousness were spent in anxiety and terror. I can't remember who told me that it was the metastases in his brain that were triggering a fright and flight response, and I clung on to the idea that if his illness had taken a different turn, he would have been able to go peacefully. "Died in his sleep, surrounded by family," as they say. I wonder, now, if that image of the ideal death is not a great lie, that most people that die "in their sleep," die, like my father, sedated, anaesthetised. That his terror had nothing to do with where his terminal illness was located, but with the fact that he knew he was dying, that finally he was perceiving, viscerally and inevitably, the coming of his death.

My dad was the one person in my life that I was certain would always have my back. He was my biggest fan. He always made sure I knew he loved me. Considering the demons he had to wrestle with himself, the amount of love and support he was able to give me was impressive. He was one of those people who try to be circuit-breakers, that decide that a long line of intergenerational trauma stops with them. He didn't quite succeed but I think he did a good job, considering.

My dad had always been told that his emotions were a sickness. His parents, for reasons of their own, were unable to understand let alone nurture him. As a teenager, my dad was sent to a psychiatric facility and given insulin shock therapy. According to dad, it was because he had made a painting of dancing skeletons. Perhaps he, like me, was grappling with thoughts of death.

My grandparents never stopped believing that my father was "mad" and needed curing. It is only now that I have come to see that the narrative of depression running in the family, of that ailment that set us apart but also made us special, the flip-side of the coin of intelligence, was a way of articulating neurodivergence. The age-old, "yes, grandpa was given to dark moods, too," family story.

Neurodivergence is said to be genetic and heritable, so like many late-diagnosed neurodivergent people, I now look at my family in a new light. My mother's autism diagnosis made so much sense of my relationship to her. I remember mum and I joking that dad was "a little bit autistic," because of his antipathy to socialising. Except as a young man, as far as I understand, he was often very outgoing. He was incredibly imaginative and creative. I think art school was a concession by my grandparents, perhaps an admission of defeat, to what they believed was mental illness.

My dad and I used to make plaster-casts of the plastic inserts in chocolate boxes. The shapes that came out looked like mini cakes, or gemstones, especially when we'd painted them with water colours. As a child I'd want to keep every bit of oddly shaped packaging. It became a joke between us, every time we had packaging to throw out, one of us would say, no, don't throw it out, we need to cast it in plaster!

I don't know what diagnosis my father would have according to the scale by which we measure such things today, but I'm pretty sure he would been deemed neurodivergent. He identified as suffering from depression, just like I did for a long time. He clearly also suffered from anxiety, but that wasn't acknowledged as distinct from depression. I think my mother and her desire to diagnose and treat, to reduce things to that simplicity, kept him believing that there was something wrong with his mind. In the eyes of my paternal grandparents, their son marrying a doctor was a stroke of luck, a way for him to be taken care of. It came easy to my mother to fit into that role, and my father perhaps also welcomed this definition of things. He had always been told he was broken, so meeting someone who believed they could fix him, easily, with a pill, must have seemed a relief.

For as long as I can remember my father had an alarm go off for him to take his tablets. "Medication time," he'd say, every evening, "medication time!" referencing one of his favourite films, *One Flew Over the Cuckoo's Nest*. He'd take SSRIs and benzodiazepines. That kept him swimming, or at least floating with his nose above water. He used to joke about taking his own life in imaginative ways, dying in a blaze of glory in some way. He was a great fan of Hunter S. Thompson.

I can't say it didn't scare me, him talking like that, but I think I kind of knew he wouldn't—partly because he wouldn't want to hurt me (he may have said as much). After my mother's suicide attempts when he had died, an old friend commented how my mum wasn't the one of my parents we'd thought would take their own life. It was said kind of jokingly, but I suddenly recognised my friend's fear, the sense she had of our difference, not just because of the talk of suicide, but the general idea of "madness" in my family, a narrative that I myself had perpetuated.

But I know my friend liked my dad: he was a cool guy, beautiful as a young man and still handsome in middle age. He was a skilled artist, who by the time I was in high school left his job as art director at an advertising firm to paint full time. Quitting the job was a relief for him, jokingly because he no longer wanted to "prostitute" his art, but also because he had to encounter fewer people, maybe even no people. He tried to promote himself as an artist for some years, but I could see how uncomfortable and anxious the necessary networking made him. So, he stopped trying to sell his work. He continued painting for many years, but after a minor stroke in his eye compromised his vision, he did so less and less.

I am ashamed to say I still see my dad as a failure. I add, "but he didn't sell much", after telling people my dad was a painter. That goes to the core of how I see myself as a writer, and why publishing a book may have been a factor in improving my mental "health." I had produced something that society sanctioned as sellable. Only since then have I been comfortable calling myself a writer. There are a lot of my father's paintings in the attic of my mother's house. People keep asking me what I will do with them, and I keep on saying I am still finding it hard, despite years passing since his death, to face sorting them out. People suggest I should exhibit them, perhaps only because they want to see them, but for me that's the rub with approaching the task of what to do with those paintings. What if nobody wants to buy one?

What if nobody ever publishes what I write? I have grappled with the idea of art for art's sake for a long time. What is the point of painting or writing, if nobody sees it or reads it? Perhaps rather than looking to my father for a way to stop fearing death, I should see him as a man who was at peace with creating for as long as he could, and then when he was no longer able to, content to enjoy others' art. As my dad painted less, he read more and more. He'd always read a lot, and it increasingly became what he did with his days. My dad read like a neurodivergent person. He'd get all the works by a writer he liked, then move on to the next one, following a trail of influences and intersections with those he had read.

It may have been through Hunter S. Thompson that my dad arrived at the beatnik poets and writers, Burroughs, Bukowski, Brautigan. I guess they were also the rebels of his youth, he always said he was a beatnik rather than a hippie in the sixties. He was more for playing it cool. The completed works of many beat writers lined up on his shelves. But like these men, he had a destructive side, a sense of simmering violence—although he was never physically violent with me.

I remember hearing my dad opening the door to the apartment we lived in when I was little. I run down what to me seems an interminably long hallway to greet him and he hugs me. He says he has a present for me, and I get excited. He opens his briefcase and brings out a children's book. It's one in a series that I love, about a pancake-eating bear that lives on a boat. But my excitement turns into disappointment (I can feel my face changing from a smile to a frown even now). I already have this one. I go to my room and pull it out of the shelf. "I already have this one, dad." His face changes. He throws the copy he's brought me across the room. He is angry, but I don't understand why.

When I was a child, my dad seemed quick to anger, mainly with my mother but also on occasion with me. Now, his is anger seems to me to be a response to being unable to handle his own as well as others' strong emotional reactions—to losing that cool he wanted to project. He wasn't angry at me but at himself.

The fear of emotions is all around us. We all want to be cool. Being emotional is not cool. My father tried hard not to pass on the judgement he'd faced from his parents, but the fear of feeling things ran deep in him. His experience was that being too emotional can get you hospitalised.

My father once said that one of the things he hated about working in the advertising office was when the women cried in front of him. One of the things I hated about working in an office was how bursting into tears was seen as very much the wrong response—to anything. It was a sign of weakness, in particular female weakness, sometimes of female guile, always of unreasonable sensitivity. Eye rolls and sighs, "don't get upset."

"I'm not upset," I wanted to shout, "I AM ANGRY," but that seemed to be a way to confirm all those stereotypes of the hysterical female that I was already fitting into by crying. Being upset, or so angry it was physically obvious, was being too emotional. The office is one of the places you are expected to regulate your emotions.

My mother frequently told me I was too sensitive, because she didn't understand why I was feeling what I was feeling. My father told me the same, but because he understood what I was feeling all too well.

I lost them both in the last decade, my dad to cancer and my mum to... what did I lose her too? Perhaps I never did and never would be able to connect to her because of some quirk of our genetics that set out neural wiring too much at odds with each other. Perhaps it is the circumstances of our lives that have meant that while she has shut herself away, fleeing from anxiety, I have come to reckon with my feelings. Not always because I have wanted to—I have wished for a simple cure, a pill, a daily habit, a way of life that would rid me of those feelings that are seen as too much. That feel like too much. And sometimes are too much.

I am not ashamed to take medication, but neither would I propose it as a solution for everyone. Maybe if my parents hadn't been who they were, I could have found ways to cope without the meds. But who they were also gave me the confidence and curiosity to question, many times myself, but increasingly the world. In my reckoning I have tried to acknowledge the complexity of what we feel and how we feel it. To admit the impossibility of answers and certainties. To accept the unbearable fear of and the inevitability of death. To acknowledge that I will never be happy, but that I will feel happiness again, as I will sadness, and anxiety and anger and grief. And it will be fucking awful, and also ok.

My dad and I painted together. He gave me a miniature easel, with a few dabs of oil paint. He showed me how to mix the colours, how to use the brushes and how to scrape the paint off the canvas if you made a mistake.

My dad and I drew together. He showed me how to draw perspective. He taught me the proportions of a human body that we see but don't see: how the foot is the length of the forearm. How the head is a seventh or so of the height of a person. How the eyes actually sit right in the middle of the head, although they appear at the top of the face.

My dad and I coloured in together. He told me to shade in one direction only to make the colour more even, and to crosshatch to make it more intense.

LAY OUT YOUR UNREST

www.ingramcontent.com/pod-product-compliance
Ingram Content Group UK Ltd.
Pitfield, Milton Keynes, MK11 3LW, UK
UKHW041902200625
6512UKWH00002B/132